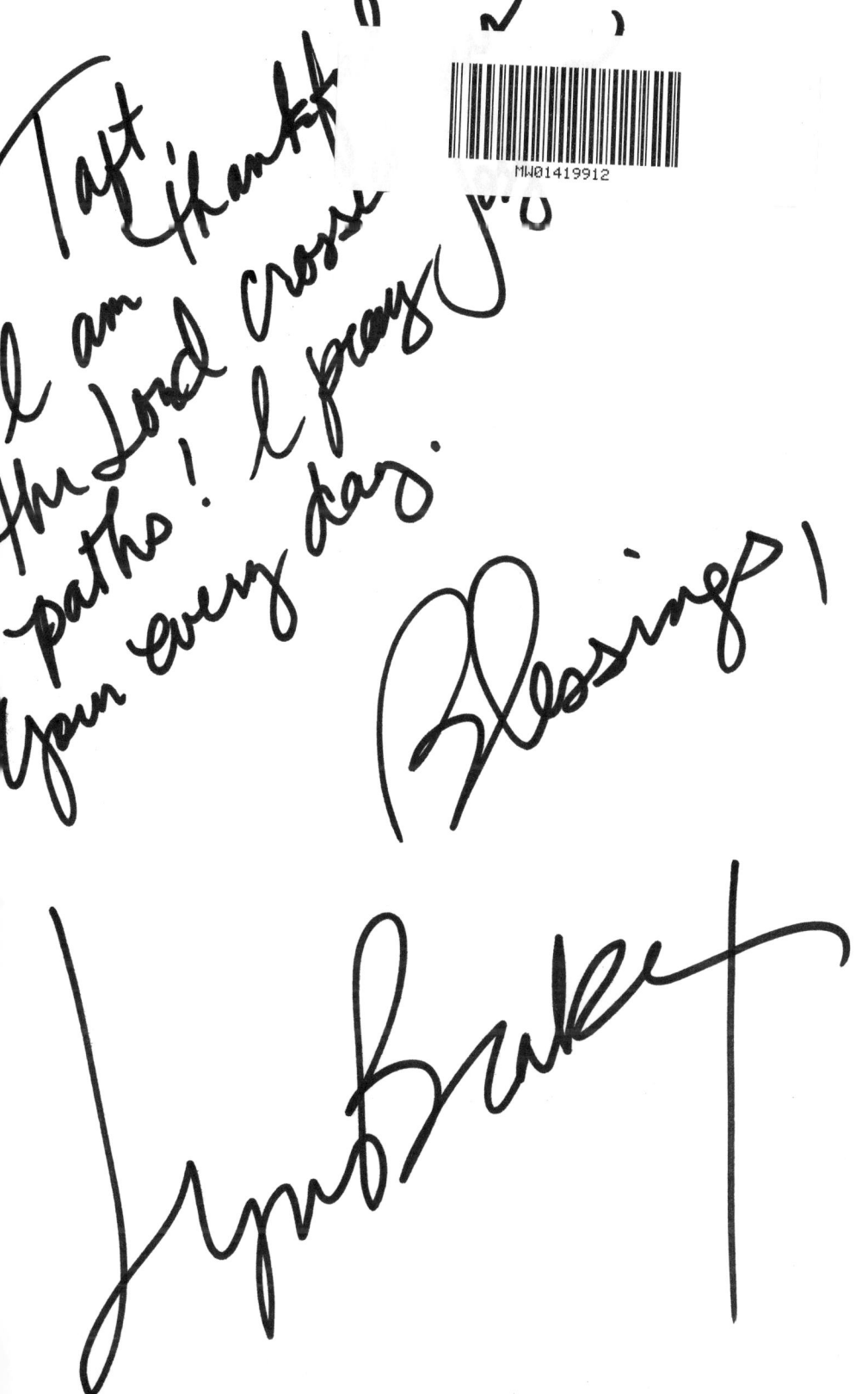

Taft "Thanks"
I am thankful the Lord crossed paths! I pray you every day.

Blessings!

Lynn Baker

THROUGH GOD'S GRACE

LYNN BRAKE

CrossBooks™
A Division of LifeWay
1663 Liberty Drive
Bloomington, IN 47403
www.crossbooks.com
Phone: 1-866-879-0502

© 2012 Lynn Brake. All rights reserved.

No part of this book may be reproduced, stored in a retrieval system, or transmitted by any means without the written permission of the author.

Scripture is taken from the Bible (New International Version). Copyright © 1973, 1978, 1984 Biblica. Used with permission of Zondervan. All rights reserved.

First published by CrossBooks 08/20/2012

ISBN: 978-1-4627-1885-6 (hc)
ISBN: 978-1-4627-1886-3 (sc)
ISBN: 978-1-4627-1887-0 (e)

Library of Congress Control Number: 2012910425

Printed in the United States of America

This book is printed on acid-free paper.

Any people depicted in stock imagery provided by Thinkstock are models, and such images are being used for illustrative purposes only.

Certain stock imagery © Thinkstock.

Because of the dynamic nature of the Internet, any web addresses or links contained in this book may have changed since publication and may no longer be valid. The views expressed in this work are solely those of the author and do not necessarily reflect the views of the publisher, and the publisher hereby disclaims any responsibility for them.

"Who would have thought that the beautiful young lady, so carefree and spirited that I met in 1979 would have to travel a path filled with such heartache? I have been given the privilege of watching Lynn grow from a lost, single college student to a spirit-filled friend, wife, mother, caregiver, and now author. If I could describe Lynn in one word it would be 'courageous'. Throughout this journey, I have witnessed how God has impacted her life on a daily basis. She has seen defeat but was never defeated. She has faced sorrow but never lost sight of where her joy came from. She has faced death but has used that experience to help others through it. This precious friend of mine has been such an example to me over the years. She has risen above the unique circumstances in her life and shown us time and time again how powerful we can be if we hold on to our faith in Christ."

Laughrie Tucker

"I have been privileged to walk with the Brakes through the struggles of cancer. I've witnessed the highs and lows of living out a faith focused on Christ. When, to the world, all seemed hopeless, I've watched this family learn more about who God is and how to rely on Him for strength, hope, and courage. The Brake family continues on their journey, learning to live out the words of Lamentations 3:22-23, "For His compassions never fail. They are new every morning."

Terry Brown
Education Pastor, Hilldale Baptist Church, Clarksville TN

"Lynn, you are such an inspiration. You updated everyone when Keith was sick so everyone could pray for him. You remained strong when you knew he wasn't going to make it, and still had the courage to smile. To see you honor God by supporting your church and attending the Passion Play just days before Keith passed, brought tears to my eyes. Knowing Jesus would be with Keith, the fact that you and the kids came to support the choir, and to praise the Lord for his endless love, was a moment I will never forget! Your light shines even through the tears. Thank you for being such a Godly woman. I am honored to call you a friend and a sister in Christ. "

Theresa Dunn

"We know of many whose lives are forever altered by a medical diagnosis. Their stories are testimonies of strength, endurance, and hope. In my years of ministry none have a more inspiring tribute of Gods faithfulness in the darkness than Keith Brake and his beautiful family. In the midst of physical pain, sorrow, and death, Keith and Lynn persevered in the hope and strength of Christ. The joy of the Lord truly is our strength! Even in the sadness of Keith's death, the peace and joy of God's presence continued to radiate in Lynn, Brittney, and Bryan. My hope is that their story will lead others to discover the hope of Christ through the darkest and most difficult trials of life."

John Thomas
Friend, Chaplain, and current teacher
of Keith's LIFE group class

"I first met Keith & Lynn Brake in the late 90's at Hilldale Baptist Church. where Keith was a deacon and adult sunday school teacher, and Lynn was a choir and praise team member. While serving on mission trips with them, I got to know more about them and their relationship with God.

When Keith first was diagnosed with leukemia I saw even more how they "trusted in the Lord.' During Keith's extended stays in the hospital I would see Lynn at church with Brittney and Bryan, and she would sing on the Praise Team and I often wondered how she did it. I soon realized it was her faith and the prayers of many that was helping carry her day after day.

Through this long journey of Keith's sickness, recovery, and the return of sickness, and then his home going, I never heard either one of them complain or ask "why is this happening to us?" Because of their relationship with their Lord and Savior, Jesus Christ, and His grace upon their lives, they had church family and friends that sat with them, cried with them, cooked and cleaned for them, and most importantly, prayed with and for them. They were able to travel this road with an amazing faith all the way to the end. Keith Brake is another soldier who has gone on to his heavenly home leaving a beautiful Christian wife who is continuing on her journey and finding joy in her mourning. Thank you for following God's call."

Brenda Barron

"I was impressed with their church's support, and their family's faith!"

Aaron Terlecki
Chaplain, Avalon Hospice, Dickson, TN

Contents

Preface xv
Chapter 1: Survivor 1
Chapter 2: Peace in the Storm 11
Chapter 3: The Beginning of the End 21
Chapter 4: Plans I Have for You 31
Chapter 5: Glimpses of Heaven 53
Chapter 6: Blessings of Easter 61
Chapter 7: Divine Assignment 69

Dedication

This book is dedicated to my husband
of twenty-nine years:

Billy Keith Brake.

It is because of your seven years of suffering through a devastating illness that the Lord gave me a foundation to reveal how He used us to speak to and reach others in order to give them hope and joy in the midst of their trials. I love you, and I can't wait till you and our child can greet me at the gates of heaven and we can forever share the glory of the Lord together.

Acknowledgments

My Lord and Savior, Jesus Christ

Brittney and Bryan Brake

Vanderbilt University Medical Center Staff

Sterling House Assisted Living Staff

Avalon Hospice

Hilldale Baptist Church Family

Rev. Verlon Moore

Paula Williams

Laughrie Tucker

Brent Parchman

Theresa Dunn

Shea Halliburton Photography

Contributors to the Leukemia and Lymphoma Society in Keith's name

The many friends and family who supported us spiritually, financially, physically, and emotionally . . . for you were the backbone of our survival

Preface

Whatever your "mourning" is—the death of a loved one, an ongoing struggle, a tragedy, a major life change, or a devastating illness—the Lord is waiting for you to call out His name so that He can bring you *joy*, no matter how sad and depressed you are. He can bring you *peace* no matter how stressed and worried you are. He can bring you *hope*, no matter how dark tomorrow seems.

If you get nothing else from this book, remember this: First, you must *believe* in the Lord, Jesus Christ. "For God so loved the world that He gave His only begotten Son, that whosoever believes in Him shall have everlasting life" (John 3:16). Then, second, you must *seek* Him in all your ways. "You will seek me and find me when you seek me with all your heart" (Jeremiah 29:13). *Wait expectantly* on the Lord to show Himself, and you will find *joy in the mourning*.

Isaiah 41:13

"For I am the Lord, your God, who takes hold of your right hand and says to you, 'Do not fear. I will help you.'"

Let me also set a foundation for this book. This is written from my perspective about my struggles, my challenges, and my tests of faith. I can write this book because of the illness that my husband suffered through, but I know he went through a much deeper challenge than I could *ever* imagine. So, as you see how I felt as we walked this road together, understand that *every* step of the way, I hurt for him, I cried for him, I prayed for him, and I sacrificed myself to keep him from further suffering. If some of my statements seem selfish, remember that behind each of those were hours, days, weeks, months, and finally years of sympathy for his every pain, suffering, and loss of who he was.

Before we begin this journey, let me honor the man my husband was before his illness took over his life and he started his journey to death here on this earth.

Keith Brake grew up a hardworking, down-to-earth young man, working the tobacco fields, hauling hay, raising horses, and managing farmland. He also became a notable captain of his high school football team. He continued that leadership role in life by becoming a manager of a well-known establishment that we all know as "Wally World," or (officially) Wal-Mart. He worked in that position for twenty years, and then he went on to manage other business establishments up until the time he was diagnosed with his illness. He also became an encouraging role model, known as "coach" to many kids in local softball, baseball, and football programs.

After he became a Christian in his early twenties, he soon became a deacon to many families as well as a Sunday school teacher, which he remained until that fateful Sunday you will read about in the coming pages. He was full of energy! He was funny, always cracking jokes and being silly just to get a laugh from those around him. He was a great practical joker, so people always looked to him for entertainment! He had a heart for people, especially the less fortunate, troubled, or those who have just had hard breaks in life. Because of that, he helped many individuals and served on large mission projects. He was always rooting for the underdog in every situation, and it was his goal to make sure people knew that God had a purpose for them, no matter where they were in life or how many mistakes they had made.

He was a friend to many people, and the Lord blessed him with more friends than you can imagine. He touched many people with his heartfelt personality, and those he touched will always carry a part of him. In the pages ahead, however, you will see how "that Keith" we all loved and cherished was soon compromised.

Jeremiah 31:13

*Then young women will dance and be glad, young men and old as well. I will turn their mourning into gladness; I will give them comfort and **joy** instead of sorrow.*

Chapter One
Survivor

My name is Lynn Brake . . . and I am a survivor. You, too, may be trying to survive a dark time in your life—the loss of a loved one, a divorce, a financial loss, a tragedy, or any major life change you have suffered. There are probably days that you feel like you just don't know how you are going to "make it." I'm praying that by the time you reach the end of this book, you will be able to join me in seeing the light, recognizing the Lord's hand in *your* situation, and finding your way out of the brokenness you are in. That is what our Lord wants to do for us. He wants to carry us through our situation and bring us out on the other side with a renewed heart, peace, and hope for the future.

Join me on my journey of being a survivor. I grew up in a broken home. My parents divorced when I was only two because my father was an alcoholic. My mom made the choice to divorce him because she wouldn't allow the abuse to continue and leave any further physical or emotional damage on me, my brother, or her. I searched for the love of a father all my life, because by all accounts, my earthly father chose not to be a part of my life after the divorce. So, as I came into adulthood, I felt a need for something deeper in my life. As I was about to head off to college,

I felt so alone, and I was. My mother had remarried and moved to Florida, and my brother had moved to Georgia . . . all within a couple of months. I now had no immediate family within miles of me. I had no one, and I knew no one in Clarksville, where I was about to attend college at Austin Peay State University. I was alone. I cried out in desperation for help, for me to make it on my own! And . . . just weeks before I was supposed to leave for college, I had a dream and was visited by what I believe was the spirit of the Lord. (Understand that at that time, I was not a Christian but had been under conviction for some time.) In that dream, I felt the power of the Lord lift me up and wrap me in His arms. I *never* in all my life felt such *unbelievable* peace, comfort, security, freedom, and mostly, pure unconditional *love* beyond understanding. He spoke to me and simply said, "Everything is going to be fine." *That* is exactly what I needed to know in that moment . . . for my future, no matter what lay ahead for me. *Little did I know—*

Eight months later, I surrendered my life to Christ at Hilldale Baptist Church in Clarksville. Reverend Verlon Moore was preaching his "trial sermon." Little did we both know, however, the Lord had set up that divine appointment. I needed to hear the "calling" from Bro. Moore's sermon that morning, and he needed one of three people to walk the aisle so that he would know this was where the Lord wanted him to serve. (You will see many more of these divine appointments throughout this book. He is an "on-time" God!)

Shortly after, the Lord crossed the paths of me and a few new friends to set the stage for His plans in my life. I began singing in the choir after I realized that the Lord had given me that gift. Through involvement in choir, a new church friend named Cindy Haley Pitts and my big sister in Kappa Delta Sorority, Laughrie Tucker, introduced me to Billy Keith Brake. Although we had only dated for a couple of months after that, Keith said that "he knew" and asked me to marry him, so we ended up getting married one year later.

Keith was also a new Christian at the time, but we both knew that we wanted to start our marriage off right and have Christ as the foundation. Little did we know at the time how profound that foundation would be for the survival of our marriage as we faced a long, difficult battle some twenty-five years later.

The first four years of our marriage were filled with working, teaching, finishing school, playing church sports, and trying to stay afloat financially so that we could build a life together. I got my degree from APSU two years after we were married. I was determined to survive so that I could be the first one in my immediate family to graduate from college and prove to those naysayers that I could do it. As a new manager of Wal-Mart, Keith faced challenges of his own in that area, and he almost made me a widow just one short month after we were married. On his first weekend to man the store alone, two men came in and overpowered the office clerk and then lured Keith into the office and overpowered him. They held a gun to his head. They bound and gagged both the employees, and threatened to shoot them unless they could escape. They escaped, and Keith survived. And he was able to come home that night! Thank you, Lord!

We moved on, thanking the Lord for His blessings, and he started teaching Sunday school for first graders. Little did we know that we would be teaching for the remainder of our marriage, not just elementary but in the youth department and then an adult class. That adult class would play an important role in our lives.

After I landed a job as a design artist and Keith began to move up financially in his position at Wal-Mart, we felt secure enough to purchase our first home! Keith worked long hours but always found time and strength to work diligently on our yard and new home. And it wasn't long after that when we discovered we were expecting a baby!

Not knowing the details of the pregnancy yet, Keith dreamed one night that it was a girl and we had named her Brittney. Two weeks later, we discovered that his dream was true, and of course, it was easy to pick her name—Brittney Lynn Brake. She was a beautiful, black-headed, blue-eyed doll. There was no doubt that she was the apple of her daddy's eyes, and there was an unspeakable bond between them from that moment on. She was forever forward a "daddy's girl!"

Four years later, we were pregnant again! We wanted our children fairly close together in age, so we were excited. It was close to Christmas when we found out about the pregnancy, so we planned a big announcement to the family on Christmas day! Everyone was so excited until the following week when we went for our checkup. There was no heartbeat. Less than a week later on New Year's Day, we miscarried. We were both devastated! For months, I felt a hole in my heart, an emptiness. A part of me was gone! Keith, though hurting, helped to pick me up and survive the situation, because we knew the Lord had a wonderful new plan for us and our family. That He did!

Six months after the miscarriage, we were pregnant again. Although reserved about the news, we held out hope, and nine months later, a precious and healthy baby boy was born—Bryan Keifer Brake. And just like Keith had that bond with Brittney, I had a "mama's boy" who clung to my side! Life was good, and we were complete.

We were determined to bring the kids up in a Christian home and environment. Neither Keith nor I had had a strong Christian foundation growing up, but we discovered as young adults how our faith in Christ brought us peace for each day, hope for our future, strength for our trials, and love that no human could provide. We wanted that for our children, so before their teenage years, both Brittney and Bryan gave their lives to Christ. Their decision would play a vital part in surviving one of the biggest trials of their lives.

As a family, we had a somewhat typical life over the coming years, with all the trials, fun, stresses, and laughter that accompanied the average American experience. We had survived a couple of serious car wrecks, surgeries for all four of us, a move to a new house, job changes, and a few major financial struggles.

The kids grew and became involved in different activities and sports. Keith and I also became more involved in church and community activities. He was appointed one of the youngest deacons in our church, and then he was chosen to coach a middle school football team and girls softball league. I was playing on a volleyball league, appointed to several church committees, and became heavily involved with our church music program. Needless to say, we were a family on the go, and loved it that way!

As the years went by and the kids reached middle and high school age, Keith and I backed off our involvement and dedicated our time to Brittney and Bryan and their activities. We understood that family was precious, life was short, and they would be leaving the nest soon. Up to this point, life seemed fairly normal and accepting. Then, of course, those teenage years, dating years, driving years, and college decisions for the kids were upon us. All I could say was, "Heaven, help us!" Although I can honestly say we were blessed with wonderful children, that phase did not come without challenges and trials.

You see, I had relied on the Lord and trusted Him through all things in my adult life, and I felt that I had developed amazing strength with Him that allowed me to overcome life's trials. Every time I faced one of the difficult phases in my life, I thought back to that dream with the Lord and reminded myself that He told me that "everything would be fine." Now that feeling was really going to be put to the test. It would be a test of faith to see if I truly trusted the Lord's promise. Believe me, there was about to be a life change that would see if I truly understood what that phrase meant, and on how many levels I would understand. I thought I had grown strong at that point! At that time, I didn't know what the word "strength" was going to mean in the coming days, months, and years.

When this "life change" took place, our children were older. Brittney was seventeen, and Bryan was twelve. Keith was forty-five then. He had gone to the doctor for a few blood tests, thinking he might have had some heart issues. The doctor called us within an hour of getting the blood tests back and said to me, "You need to get Keith to the hospital as soon as possible. We are admitting him for blood transfusions." I was puzzled. Why would he need transfusions? The doctor then said, "We will explain when you get here."

We arrived, and he was immediately admitted to the hospital. We endured a flurry of doctors and staff and tests over the next twenty-four hours. The doctor made a declaration to me at the end of the twenty-four hours and a night's stay in the hospital—a statement that would set our world on a different path. He said, "Your husband has myelodysplastic syndrome."

What on earth was that? I thought. I would come to know that word well. It was a form of leukemia, a blood cancer. Talk about devastated, shocked, and scared—Thus, the stages of true survival and strength began!

Over the next seven years, Vanderbilt University Medical Center in Nashville became our second home. Keith was in and out of the hospital for weeks, which turned into months. He underwent blood tests, blood transfusions, every test and exam imaginable. During all of this, we learned that Keith needed a bone marrow or a stem cell transplant. Without it, he would not survive but a few months at best. He was surviving, and I was surviving. We ran on autopilot, and we lived in a constant state of shock; however, we were surviving. I knew the Lord had a purpose for this, but I didn't fully understand it yet. On some level, I knew that He would use this process to show others how faith was carrying us each day.

Then came the waiting while they researched the National Bone Marrow Registry, and we soon learned the cost of this procedure! How were we going to financially survive this—*if* they found a match at all. Through the prayers of friends and family, donations and fund-raisers were being planned. God had answered those prayers. Even though we both considered ourselves self-sufficient and didn't rely on help from others, we soon learned we had to let our pride go and trust in the good hearts of friends and family to get us through this ordeal. We soon saw that this charity came as a direct result of the Lord's grace in our lives. We trusted that He would take care of us. We had to!

Then with the news of a matched donor, there came two forms of chemo to prepare for the stem cell transplant. (It was a MUD transplant, which means matched unrelated donor. Thank you, donor from Europe, for helping to keep my husband alive.) After the transplant, we had to stay close to Vanderbilt for a hundred days, and we ended up in a "medical apartment" for another month and a half until they knew that Keith wouldn't reject the stem cells. During that time, I tried to keep that apartment supplied and functioning, with someone staying with Keith 24-7 in case he suddenly developed a fever. He was so susceptible to infection at the time. I also tried to be at home in Clarksville, a forty-mile drive away from the medical apartment so that I could be there for the kids. Brittney was a senior in high school, and Bryan was in his first year of middle school. I wanted their life to be as normal as possible. Again, I didn't know the strength that would develop within me and where that strength would come from.

That strength would continue to develop and sustain me and Keith through the days ahead. We knew from the beginning of this journey that Keith could develop an infection that would take over his body within hours and that he could die. We both had to prepare our hearts and our minds for that. Every day from that day forward, we had to be ready to accept that fact. We stayed on constant guard and preparedness, never allowing ourselves to venture too far from Vanderbilt just in case. We learned to survive emotionally, physically, and spiritually one day at a time.

As the years progressed, Keith endured many surgeries. As a result of the unrelated donor, there were many complications and side effects, which resulted in mitral heart valve surgery, cataract surgery, complete dental extraction of all teeth, a fitting for dentures, gallbladder surgery, many bone marrow biopsies, PICC line insertions, port insertions, and the list goes on. But he was living.

The Lord's mercy allowed Keith to live for seven more years, giving Bryan time to grow into a young man who could mature and grow deeper in his Christian faith. Brittney was able to deepen her Christian walk during that time as well. They became a support system for one another during one of their darkest trials to come.

God's grace saw us all through many dark days, financial uncertainties, marriage trials, depression, and days when we wanted to give up, but we held on because we were believers, because we had faith in the Lord, because we knew that no matter what tomorrow held, we knew *who held tomorrow.*

Isaiah 35:10

*And those the LORD has rescued will return. They will enter Zion with singing;
everlasting **joy** will crown their heads.
Gladness and **joy** will overtake them, and sorrow and sighing will flee away.*

Chapter Two
Peace in the Storm

And tomorrow came.

On March 20, 2011, Keith was supposed to show up at church to teach Sunday school, which he had done for the past thirty years. However, twenty-five minutes into class time, he was not there. That was not like Keith. He was always early everywhere he went. Twenty-five minutes turned into an hour and then two hours. He was officially . . . missing. Needless to say, I was a basket case. You see, I had a feeling why he was now considered missing.

Let me back up to a few months before this date. Even though for the past seven years, I had witnessed Keith go through physical, emotional, and mental changes and irrational behavior because of the medications and side effects of the transplant and surgeries, there were different changes going on with him that I just could not put my finger on. He was acting more different than ever before, and his memory was "going south" quickly. (He couldn't even remember that Bryan, his own son, had just graduated from high school.) He could not put thoughts together in a normal fashion, and his rationality began to resemble that of a ten- or twelve-year-old. Even though most people who were around him in small doses did not recognize these traits, I saw the symptoms more and more every day over a six-month period.

As time got closer and closer to that day on March 20, all of these traits began to increase on a daily basis. By this point, though, I was just about at my wits' end. I was forced to keep daily tabs on his whereabouts for his own safety, even though that made him angrier each day. I would have to follow up on his every decision and "undo" some of the damage done, whether it was financial, things said to others, or plans made with others that I knew couldn't happen.

Two weeks before March 20, others close to him began question me about changes they saw in him. That alone was a relief, because I had carried that burden on my shoulders and did not share details with anyone. I felt like others would view these concerns and complaints as a "marriage valley" and that I just needed to be a big girl and "deal with it!"

At the point of Keith's original diagnosis seven years prior, I knew that his illness would either make or break our marriage, as most traumatic incidents in life can and will. Even though our marriage had all the typical stresses and everyday struggles to keep the spark alive, for the past seven years of his illness, the dynamics of our marriage changed. (*That* alone could be a whole other book.) Even though there were times when I felt I couldn't take any more of the stress from all the medical changes, personality changes, and marital changes—the human side of me wanted to throw my hands up and walk away—I knew that as a Christian, I just couldn't do that. I made a vow to the Lord almost thirty years prior that that I would stay by his side "in sickness and in health." Little did I know at the time I made those vows just how deep that statement would challenge me and my faith. Honestly, by this time, seven years after he had been diagnosed, I was tired mentally, physically, and emotionally.

As those two weeks progressed, Keith got worse and worse mentally. More people outside our immediate circle were starting to see and question his mental status. Yet, I was still reluctant to share and vent my frustrations about Keith, thinking they would "blow it off" as just more marriage challenges. I felt this storm brewing all around me, and I was getting more and more scared, frustrated, and desperate. I prayed and cried out to the Lord, "*Please*, please, please tell me what to do. I can't take any more of this." I knew that Psalm 107 promised that "if we cry out to the Lord in our troubles, He would deliver us from our stress." I just needed Him to deliver us *now*.

As days passed and Keith got worse, he would dress himself strangely or leave the faucet running and walk away. He would get up in the middle of the night and feel his way down the walls, as if he was in a strange house searching for doorways to get out. He got his days mixed with nights, and his nights with days, thinking it was time to get ready to go to Sunday morning church at night.

I began questioning his driving abilities, and I would offer to drive us everywhere. However, Keith Brake did not like anyone else to drive, so that itself would stir up a confrontation. But I was still scared for him to get behind the wheel and risk injury to himself and others. All these things were now happening every day.

Once again, I only shared these things with very few people. Even though this storm continued to brew around me, I kept it to myself to the point that I thought I was the one going crazy. I didn't have an explanation for these changes. Keith had not been to the doctor for a checkup in a couple of months, and he put up a fight at the very suggestion to get checked out. Again, I continued to cry out to the Lord, literally crying at this time, "*Please*, please, please, Lord, tell me what to do. I can't take the weight of this stress anymore. Take this burden from me and tell me what is going on!" I knew the Bible said in John 14:27, "Peace I leave with you; my peace, I give to you. Not as the world gives do I give to you. Let not your heart be troubled, neither let them be afraid." But I was. When was the Lord going to hear my cry?

Then the morning of March 20 came. At first, it seemed like every other Sunday morning, with the exception of his strange behavior, so I proceeded to get ready for church. As I checked in on him, I quickly noticed that this day seemed worse than others. I walked in, and he had put his clothes on backward and inside out. He tried to put his false teeth in upside down, but he would have brief moments of clarity, too. When I was hovering over him and trying to fix the things he was doing backward, he became quickly irritated and mad. He began to scream and accuse me of treating him like a child, like an idiot. So I backed off. And when I tried to convince him to let me drive us to church, he would have *nothing* to do with *that*! In fact, he proclaimed (and stuck to it) that *he* was driving himself to church. He told me to go on ahead and that he would be there shortly. I still continued to convince and manipulate the situation to change his mind, but the more I did that, the madder he got until he screamed for me to leave! So, with extreme reluctance, I did.

I was a nervous wreck by this time, shaking all over. I felt like I was on the verge of a breakdown. I was distraught, not knowing what to do. I left the house, scared to death, but I headed to church. I was in a panic and torn. I began calling friends in our Sunday school class to so that they could keep a lookout for him. I told them that that he was acting extremely strange and disoriented. That morning, I had no choice but to share what had been developing and increasing for months, no matter how "it looked" to others. I was at the end of my rope, and I needed help and support. Once I got to church, I quickly found one of our pastors and told him to watch for Keith because he wasn't acting right. I went to choir to sing for our first service, all the while worrying and watching for Keith from the choir loft, knowing that if I could just lay eyes on him, I would know that he had arrived safely. But he never arrived. And little did I know at the time that he would never *walk* back through the doors of our church again, something that had played a *huge* part of our thirty years together. It was gone.

Under normal circumstances Keith was ALWAYS early to everything. So, it was totally out of character for him when twenty minutes of class had passed and he had not arrived. For him not to be there to lead his class would have been very unacceptable in his eyes, so we were all left bewildered and scared for his safety. Then we all started calling his phone, then calling family and friends to see if they had seen or heard from him. Many friends started hitting the street looking for him. Two hours passed, and I was an absolute basket case, sobbing uncontrollably! I knew . . . I just knew something was very wrong. See, I had an understanding of the situation that hardly anyone else had. But that secret I had kept for so long was now being revealed and spreading like wildfire. Even though I was panicking and desperate, I felt a sense of relief and freedom that I didn't have to carry that secret anymore. I didn't have to carry that burden on my shoulders anymore, and everyone all around me was starting to see and understand that what was going on was much bigger than just a "marriage valley." It was real, and it was serious.

Near the end of the two-hour ordeal, through the intervention of a friend who contacted the police department to put out a BOLO report (to be on the lookout for a missing person because of certain medical conditions), we received a call. The police department called to say they had found a man who fit the description of the report and that he had been involved in an accident and had been taken to our local hospital. He was all right physically, but he was very disoriented. In that moment, I was relieved, but I still knew that I was about to get news, very uncertain news. Still, all the way to the hospital, I was praying and praising and thanking Jesus that He had kept my husband safe, that he hadn't hurt anyone else in the process.

When we arrived at the hospital, I was met by the police, who questioned me and explained what had happened. They explained that he had had an accident in a big intersection of town, ran a red light, and T-boned with another truck. The accident had taken place miles away from the church, where he was supposed to be. I couldn't understand why he had ended up down there, and even when the police questioned him, Keith said he didn't know why he was there. "He was just looking for his mom," . . . who had passed away two and a half years earlier! It turned out to be a minor accident that hurt no one in the process (what I believe was God's 'hedge of protection' around Keith and the other person involved). Because Keith was disoriented and acting abnormal, the police thought he had been intoxicated or had hit his head on impact! That alone led the hospital to do a head CT scan. *That* scan would change all our lives.

That scan revealed that Keith had lesions on his brain. I knew it was very serious, and I knew this might have been the end, the "it" that we had been warned about seven years ago, the "it" that at any moment would lead to his death. Once we were given the results, I knew we were about to face a challenge like none we had faced in the past seven years, as difficult and challenging as they were. But as the hours passed that afternoon as he was prepared to be transferred to Vanderbilt Hospital, in the midst of this huge storm that had been brewing for weeks and in the midst of the trauma and uncertainty of that day, I suddenly realized that the Lord had answered my cries for help from the weeks past.

During all these weeks, I had been carrying the burden of the mental and emotional changes of Keith, afraid to share them so that I could protect his dignity and the personal state of our marriage. During all these weeks, I knew something was seriously wrong medically with Keith, but his visits to the hospital had not alerted us to anything serious. I realized He had answered all my questions and cries for help. Because of the two-hour window when Keith had been missing, everyone quickly learned about what had been going on for months now. I didn't have to carry *that* burden. The accident had taken place (without any injuries), and it had led to the scan that revealed *why* Keith had demonstrated this strange behavior. There were lesions making him act that way. The Lord had heard me. He had heard my cries and answered them without me forcing Keith to see the doctor or without me solving the problems myself. He did it! So, in those hours and the events of the day, with this storm brewing all around me, I suddenly realized that I had *peace*, a peace I hadn't experienced since that dream years earlier, a peace that even I didn't understand. And I knew, because He knew my heart and knew my hurt and my cries and my pain. I knew that even though the days ahead looked dark, He was there with me, with us, and that He would carry us through every single moment. I was at peace. I had peace in the midst of the storm.

Philippians 4:6-7

Do not be anxious about anything, but in everything, by prayer and petition, with thanksgiving, present your requests to God. And the peace of God, which transcends all understanding, will guard your hearts and your minds in Christ Jesus.

Psalm 94:19

*When anxiety was great within me, your consolation brought me **joy**.*

Chapter Three
The Beginning of the End

There was a challenge ahead of us now that would strengthen our bond beyond words. We didn't know how long or how short this journey was going to be, but we knew it was going to be the most difficult challenge we had faced. I knew that it was going to be a long haul and that I would need the prayers of others.

Around then, I had been handed a CD to listen to on my drives back and forth to the hospital (a forty-mile trek). The Lord knew that He could speak to me through music, because it was where my heart of worship was. Little did this person know that a song on this CD would turn out to be *the* song that would help give me and my daughter the power and energy and strength to keep going. Because the Lord had just shown me "peace in the midst of my storm" and released me from the bondage of suffering and given me peace, this song shared that moment of "freedom" I had experienced. I had heard the song by another artist several times before, but when I really "heard" it for the first time, I wept because I knew the Lord had sent this song to me. The words identified the sufferings I had gone through for so long. In the same moment, this song spoke to me by confirming that even in the darkest moment of one's life, I should still *praise*

Him through my circumstance. He had it all under control, and He was taking care of us despite our coming loss. The song is called "Shackles" by Mary Mary. (See the entire song lyrics at www.songlyrics.com.)

In the corners of my mind, I just can't seem to find
a reason to believe that I can break free,
I have been down for so long, Feels like
all hope is gone,
But as I lift my hands, I understand that
I should praise you
through my circumstance.
Everything . . . all went wrong at one time,
I thought I was gonna lose my mind.
I need you to lift this load, 'cause I can't take anymore.
Been through the fire and rain, bound in
every kind of way,
But God has broken every chain, so let me go!

This song was yet confirmed by the scripture I Thessalonians 5:16-18:

Rejoice always, pray continually, give thanks in all circumstances: for this is God's will for you in Christ Jesus.

And I'll praise you in this storm and I will lift my hands for You are who You are no matter where I am. And every tear I've cried You hold in your hand. You never left my side, and though my heart is torn, I will praise You in this storm.

About a week into the hospital stay at Vanderbilt, a special friend (who would later take Keith's place as teacher in the Sunday school class) prayed with me in the hall outside Keith's room and said to me, "Lynn, you know that the Lord is going to use this journey to touch people's lives on so many levels that we won't even be aware of?" I knew the Lord could and that He probably would. I just didn't know whom He would touch or how or when. And really, that wasn't for me to be concerned with. I knew he was working through us and our situation to speak to others, and He had a plan for everyone involved. The weeks to come, though, would certainly reveal some of the answers to those questions.

Through the first few weeks in Vanderbilt, we were uncertain of the definite diagnosis. Therefore, because we did not know what the outcome of this journey would be, we had to rely on our faith that the Lord was in control and that He would take care of us. We all want the end result of everything in our lives to be perfect and normal. We want our loved ones to live and remain in perfect health. We want our marriages to be successful and full of unconditional love. We want our relationships to be healthy. We want our careers to be fulfilling and successful and our finances to always flourish. The truth of the matter is that we live in an imperfect world, so that is the reason that our faith is so important. With our faith in the Lord, we have hope and certainty that through all of these imperfect outcomes, we are going to be just fine. Someone shared the following with me: "Faith is not about everything turning out okay. Faith is about being okay, no matter how things turn out."

When you face uncertain times, it is good—in some cases, it's a necessity—to have friends and loved ones by your side for support and encouragement. The Lord never intended for us to walk difficult journeys alone. The Lord places people in our lives as His instruments: prayer warriors, providers, and encouragers to help us cope through the hard times. It was those people who blessed us with overflowing support: financially with gas and food, supplies for the hospital rooms, gifts to help us cope with the long hours and days at the hospital. We had people who constantly volunteered to sit with Keith at night so I could go home and get rest to make it through the next day. We had friends taking care of my car and Keith's truck, and they were helping with delivering bills, picking up mail, and so on! The stream of loved ones and visitors was endless. Vanderbilt staff said they have never seen such support for any one patient before! I can honestly say that I did not want for much during Keith's seven weeks in the hospital. That was a testament of the love many had for Keith, me, and the kids. It was a testament of God's love flowing from His people. I never had a day that I wasn't overwhelmed with His grace!

Then, one day at the hospital the doctors pulled me aside to confirm all their findings. The lesions were most definitely brain cancer. Without any further doubt, I knew instantly that Keith's days were numbered. The doctors had confirmed my instincts from that day on March 20, that this was the 'beginning of the end'. We were looking at anywhere from two to six weeks . . . at best.

I began to share the news that Keith was not going to make it with everyone who had come to visit. As friends and family began to receive the news of Keith's numbered days, I became the comforter to so many because the Lord had already showered me with peace and comfort through the prayers of others. I did not have the capacity and physical strength to bathe this situation in prayer 24-7. That is when the intervention and intercessory prayers of others filled me with the strength I needed . . . so much that I realized one day at the hospital that I had become the comforter. 2 Corinthians 3-5 explains how that happens. I knew that was written in God's word, but I had never seen it lived out right before my eyes!

You should realize that I had known the news for over a week before I shared it with my kids, family, and friends. One by one, as people streamed in, I broke the news to them, and I found myself hugging them, wiping their tears, and letting them know that it was okay. And it was. I knew the Lord was holding us in

His hands, taking care of us, and I knew that Keith was going to be free of pain and suffering now and that he would be at the right hand of the Father in heaven. There would be peace. Then one day, one of Keith's best friends came in, knowing I would have to share the news. I braced myself for his reaction. And it was the same as most everyone else. As he wept in my arms, he suddenly stood up and said through his tears, "I am so embarrassed! I am supposed to be comforting you and look at you. *You* are comforting *me!* It's not right!"

And without hesitation, the Lord supplied me with the words to give him, and I said, "It is right. I have been bathed in prayer over this until my cup runneth over! I have been given a strength that can only come from the Lord. Because I have enough to supply my needs, I have enough to share with you. It is right!"

2 Corinthians 1:3-4

Praise be to the God and Father of our Lord Jesus Christ, the Father of compassion and the God of all comfort, who comforts us in all our troubles, so that we can comfort those in any trouble with the comfort we ourselves receive from God.

It was during this time that I understood the Lord's strength on a physical level. I am one who always treasured and needed a good seven hours of sleep each night and sometimes a quick nap in the afternoons just to function. If that didn't happen, I was collapsing from no energy by the next afternoon, or I couldn't function or think straight. Even though over the seven years of Keith's illness I learned to adapt to strange hours of sleep, I always managed to get sufficient sleep during his hospital stays and unsettling nights at home. Under the circumstances of knowing what the outcome of this situation was going to be, I was spending as many waking hours as possible with Keith . . . and when I couldn't, sleep didn't come easy. So, at one point, during this long . . . and last . . . hospital stay, I had gone for 3 solid days without hardly any sleep. By the end of the third day, I discovered an overflowing strength that I did not understand. I was functioning normally!!! This was so 'not like me' to have this strength, especially after three straight days without a normal night's sleep. I remember sitting down for a moment on the afternoon of that third day, and said to a friend in the room with me, "I don't know how in the world I am functioning right now with the lack of sleep over these last three days." And in that moment that I uttered those words, the revelation hit me . . . and I began to weep out of gratitude toward the Lord, because I knew, in that moment, that Lord had, once again, and through the intercessory prayers of others, followed through on His promise in Isaiah 40:29, 31.

Isaiah 40:29-30

It is He who gives strength to the weary, and it is He who increases fortitude and strength in those who are failing ... But those who hope in the Lord will renew their strength. They will take up wings like eagles. They will run and not grow weary. They will walk and not be faint.

2 Samuel 22:33

It is God who arms me with strength and keeps my way secure.

Jeremiah 29:11

*"For I know the plans I have for you," declares the LORD,
"plans to prosper you
and not to harm you, plans to give you hope
and a future."*

Chapter Four
Plans I Have for You

It's easy to get discouraged when things are going bad, but we shouldn't lose heart because God is at work in our lives, even in the midst of our pain and suffering. He is already at work, planning and paving the way to take care of us long before our circumstances arrive. Remember the next time you seem to be "crashing and burning," it may just be the smoke signal that summons the grace of God.

These stories are only a few of the many interventions that the Lord wove into our lives. As we began to see these results unfold during Keith's time in the hospital, we felt the peace and reassurance that we were being taken care of in the midst of what should have seemed like a devastating time. These interventions showed us just how much God loved us and that He would take care of every detail for our lives. And it gave us a hope that even though we were traveling through this dark valley we were going to be okay, too.

Matthew 6:34

*Therefore do not worry about tomorrow, for tomorrow will worry about itself.
Each day has enough trouble of its own.*

Brittney: Just five months before Keith went into the hospital, Brittney had an interview for what she thought was going to be her dream job. She knew this job would possibly mean long hours and time on the road. She didn't mind sacrificing for her dream, and she was anxious to accept the position. The interview process came down to her and one other person, and the other person ended up with the job. She was crushed. We encouraged her to move past the disappointment and look to the future for another opportunity because we knew the Lord had another plan for her. And boy, did he!

As the time when Keith went into the hospital approached, Brittney had again been offered another position, but to our surprise, she turned it down. She said she had a peace that this just wasn't the right job or the right time. She soon revealed to us the Lord had told her to reject it and then gave her that peace. The Lord had a plan.

Two weeks after Keith's death, out of the blue—of course, we know now it was God's divine timing—Brittney was approached by the same organization that had interviewed her for the first job. They asked *her* to come in to interview for a position, which had more stable hours, no traveling, and a comparable salary in the field she had dreamed of. She accepted the job! On the heels of her dad's death, this job now gave her a focus and a future to look forward to!

As we looked back at the timing and provision of God's grace, we realized how He had orchestrated everything surrounding Brittney's job. He knew her dad's death was coming. We realized that had she gotten that first job months before, she may not have been able to get the time off to be with her dad during his last days. And we know, too, that the Lord gave her peace to turn down that second position because it would have been just a month or so from that time when her dad would start his journey to death. In both cases, the Lord had a plan for her. Thank you, Lord, for waiting to give her the job of her dreams . . . just when she needed it most!

Bible study group: Not only did the Lord provide for Brittney in her professional life, but He also helped with her personal life. (I am not surprised. He covers all the bases and cares about every detail.) Just four months before Keith went into the hospital that last time, Brittney's close friends decided to form a new Bible study group. Little did she know at the time that members of that group would provide a deep level of emotional support for her in the coming days.

Once the news of Keith's prognosis was apparent, Brittney soon discovered how the Lord had placed specific members of that Bible study group together to show her empathy and guidance and give her shoulders to cry on. For instance, one of the friends in the

Bible study group had previously lost one of her parents and was able to empathize and lead Brittney through the grief process. The group surrounded her and prayed over her continually through the whole process. This group, along with other close friends, came together and donated money so that Brittney could take as much time off from work as needed without the worry and stress of losing funds to cover her bills. The Lord is there to resolve every concern when we go through trials.

Bryan: In the fall before Keith's diagnosis, Bryan had left for college in Chattanooga. Upon arrival, he became heavily involved in a Christian organization called Young Life. Because most of his friends had scattered after high school graduation, the Young Life group had quickly developed into a close-knit second family for him. By the time Keith went into the hospital in March, Bryan had been chosen and named a Young Life leader who ministered to high school kids in the Chattanooga area. Being chosen as a leader automatically connected him to a larger network of other leaders who became a vital part of Bryan's support system during Keith's last days and the funeral. In fact, Bryan had about thirty members who drove almost three hours to support him on the day of the funeral, even though he had only been named a leader a few weeks prior to leaving school so that he could come home to be with his dad. Because this bond had developed in less than seven months' time, we fully saw how God orchestrated their paths to cross just months before Bryan would need them. It was their love and support that became a huge part of carrying Bryan through the pain of his father's death.

John Thomas: One of Keith's requests since the day he had been first diagnosed seven years earlier was that when something happened to him, he wanted his Sunday school class to remain together at all costs. Our class had been together for years and had developed a very tight bond. Before Keith's final diagnosis, our longtime friend John Thomas, who was a former pastor, had recently become a beloved member of our Sunday school class. Keith asked him to substitute for him during each of his frequent hospital stays that fell on Sundays. Because John was no longer serving in the pastoral role, the opportunity for him to step up and lead our class in Keith's absence was just what John needed to find a purpose and opportunity to share his teaching gift and leadership abilities.

The year before Keith's final hospital stay, John and his wife had to move to another church for a short job opportunity. We were happy for them but saddened that he had lost John from our class. But the Lord once again had a plan. John and his wife returned to our class just weeks before Keith went into the hospital for his final stay. This was definitely God's divine timing! Without any question or concern about who would teach Keith's class, John stepped in to keep the class going.

One day, after Keith's final diagnosis was known to all, John was in the hospital room visiting. Our conversation was about Keith's absence and ultimate vacancy as the teacher for his beloved Sunday school class. In a moment of clarity for Keith, he spoke up and pointed at John and said, "Him! Him! There's your Sunday school teacher!" As a result of Keith's 'divine appointing', and the overwhelming agreement from the class members, John permanently stepped into this role for Keith. This provision fulfilled Keith's wishes to keep his class intact no matter what!

The Lord also involved John in one of the most important events surrounding Keith's death—his funeral. Although we knew we would have a couple of pastors be part of the funeral service, all of whom had been a very important part of our lives, there was no doubt in Keith's mind who would preach the main part of the service. Many probably expected that one of the other pastors would play that important role, but not in Keith's eyes. He chose John Thomas, the least likely candidate. Keith was always for the "underdogs," the ones who had been through difficult times and couldn't see their purpose for the future. After John had returned to church following some difficult trials in his life, Keith approached him and said, "Lift your chin up. God still has a purpose for you!" Keith wanted to use this story to send a message at his funeral—the Lord takes the broken and downhearted and refines them and uses them for His good and His purpose, no matter what mistakes or wrong turns they have made in life! And He did use John in a big way to share this story at the funeral. There were over a thousand people who heard the Lord's message of forgiveness!

My mother: My mother had been diagnosed with Alzheimer's two years prior to the time that Keith had been diagnosed with brain cancer. She had been on a continual decline and had reached the beginning of the last stage of Alzheimer's about six months before Keith had his final diagnosis. We realized that just a couple of months before Keith going into the hospital, she suddenly stopped regressing without any medicine changes. At the time, we were not sure why this change had taken place, but we were relieved that she was in a "holding position" so that we could treasure this "good place" with her. Until this point, I had been going to take care of her a couple times a week and sharing the burden of her care with my stepfather.

Once Keith went into the hospital, there was no way that I could devote that time to her, because I was consumed with Keith's illness and hospital stays, spending every possible moment with him, knowing these were his last days on this earth. I was thankful that the Lord softened the heart of my stepfather, as he graciously accepted the fact that he would have to take care of Mom on his own for a while.

As I looked back at this situation, I realize and fully believe that *this* was yet another way that the Lord showed His grace to me during this time. I fully believe that He was responsible for halting my mother's regression so that responsibility would be taken from me during Keith's dying days. At my mother's pace of regression, I knew without a shadow of a doubt that by spring of that year(the exact time of Keith's hospital stay and death), she would have regressed so much that we would have to place her in an assisted living facility. But we didn't have to because of the halt in her regression, and my stepfather was able to fully take care of her. Consequently, I didn't have to worry about that. Thank you, Lord, for taking care of that detail in *my* life.

There's another detail confirming that the Lord had His hand in this experience: Just two months after Keith's death—at the time, I was starting to breathe again, emotionally speaking—my mother's regression kicked back in when I could once again assist and be there for her.

Laughter: You would think that in these moments and days of shock and sorrow, watching your loved one decline with each passing day, you would experience a constant state of grief. However, because of our faith and because we knew that Keith would soon be free of his pain and suffering, the Lord supplied us with a constant source of smiles and laughter. Oddly enough, the source of all that laughter came from Keith! As I mentioned before, Keith was a practical joker, and he loved to make people laugh.

Well, the Lord preserved Keith's keen sense of humor until the last days of his life despite the fact that most every other avenue of his brain was deteriorating. This gift alone was a blessing of survival for the family and friends. Hardly a day went by that he didn't come up with something to make everyone laugh through their pain. For instance, he came up with "pet names" for friends, created clicking 'radar' noises directed at me, and made faces at us without his false teeth in! These were just a few of the many moments of laughter he provided for us to give us a moment of release from the seriousness and sadness surrounding us. They were most definitely moments of *joy*.

These are but a few of the many examples of how the Lord intervened to show His mighty hand at work in our trials. We began to recognize His blessings as the weeks passed. Just the recognition of the Lord's presence in these areas was enough to ease our suffering. It let us know, that just as He promised, 'He would be with us, carrying us through our trials'. Once again, the

Joy Comes in the Mourning

Lord used someone during this time to send another song to us to help recognize those blessings we had in the middle of our trials. It is simply called 'Blessings' by Laura Story. (See again, the entire song lyrics at http://www.songlyrics.com.)

We pray for blessings
We pray for peace
We pray for healing
We pray for Your mighty hand to ease our suffering
All the while, You hear each spoken need
What if your blessings come through raindrops
What if your healing comes through tears
What if a thousand sleepless nights
Are what it takes to know You're near
What if trials of this life are your mercies in disguise
What if... the aching of this life
The rain, the storms, the hardest nights
Are your mercies in disguise

A Christmas family photo, just weeks after being diagnosed with MyeloDysplastic Syndrome.

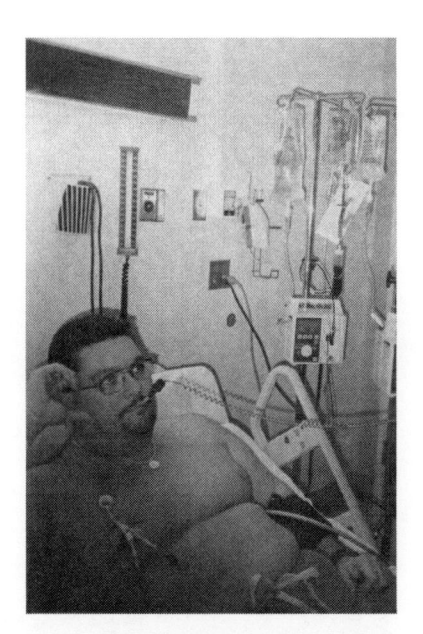

Keith at Gateway Medical Center in Clarksville,
TN within the first month of being diagnosed in November of 2003. This is his first of MANY ports receiving blood and several bags of antibiotics.

Keith and Bryan (who had just turned 12) on one of their VERY FEW visits allowed for Bryan at Vanderbilt University Medical Center in Nashville, TN while Keith was waiting on his stem cell transplant.

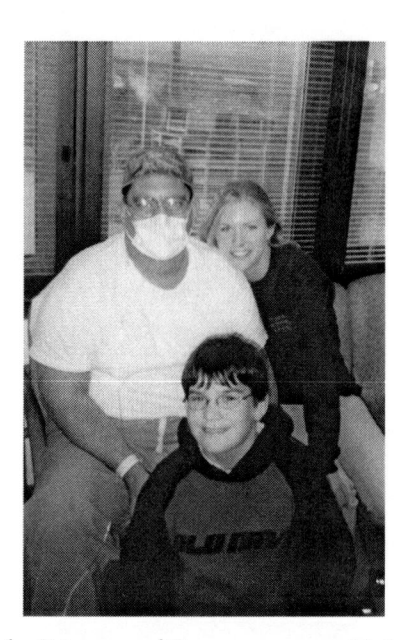

Keith, with the Brittney and Bryan, on a rare visit in the hospital before his transplant. They had to meet in the waiting room, because it was in the middle of flu season, and Bryan, being a minor, was not allowed on the transplant floor.

Joy Comes in the Mourning

Keith and his best friend, John Nichols, at Vanderbilt before his transplant.

Keith, in the days before his transplant, sporting his 'doo rag' and goofing off, as he did often to get a laugh out of everyone!

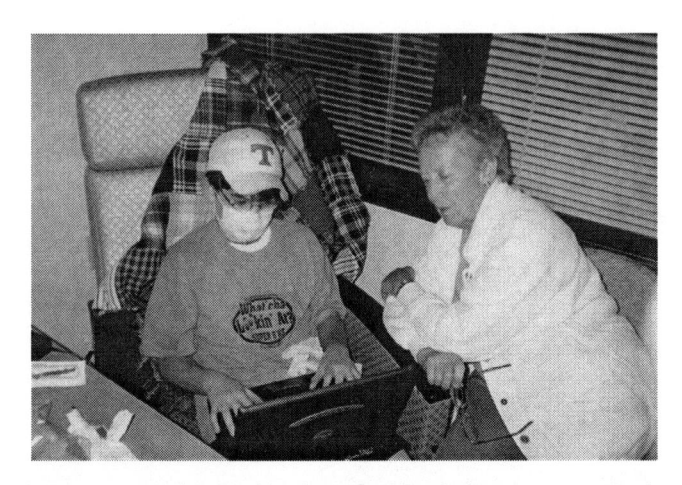

Bryan, wearing his mask to keep from spreading germs to Keith, was with granny Jean Bryan (before she was diagnosed with Alzheimer's). They were passing the time and waiting on a call from the transplant team to let us know that Keith's stem cells were being flown in.

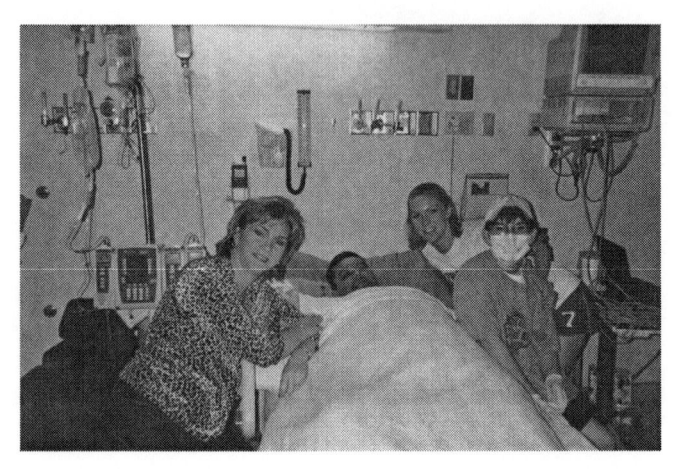

A family photo the evening of Keith's transplant on March 25, 2004. Bryan was the only one that had to wear a mask and gloves because he was a minor, and more prone to carry infections.

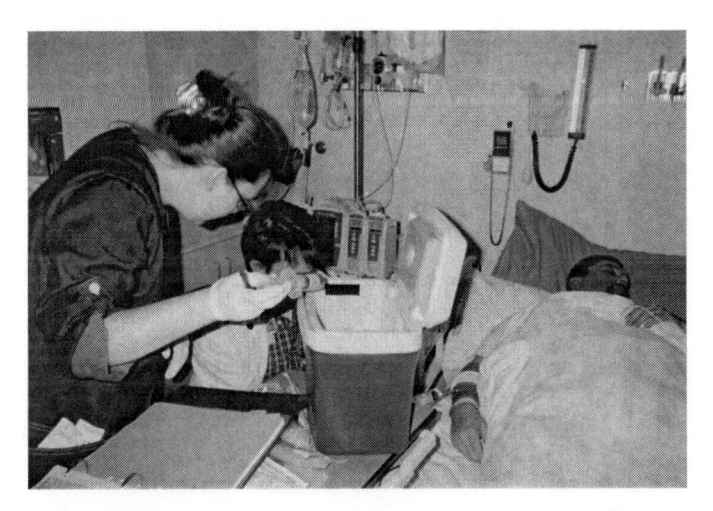

The transplant team documenting and counting stem cell vials after being flown in from overseas from Keith's donor in Europe.

Keith, in the medical apartment after his transplant, sharing a laugh with Payton Williams (or P-man, as Keith called him).

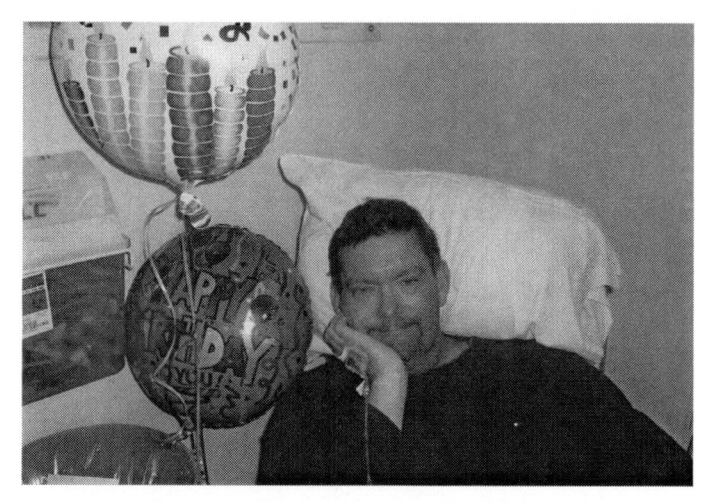

Keith celebrating one of several birthdays in his room at Vanderbilt University Medical Center.

Last Easter Sunday family photo taken almost one year to the day before Keith's death.

Keith in one of his happiest moments, when we surprised Brittney with a car for her college graduation in spring of 2009.

One of the last pictures taken of Keith with Brittney.

One of the last pictures taken of Keith with Bryan.

Keith and me at a cancer benefit dinner the November before his death.

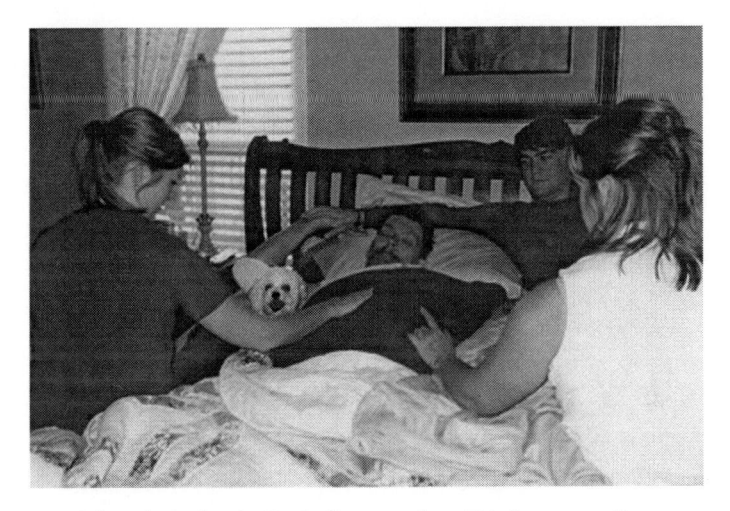

The whole family (including our dog, Toby) surrounding Keith . . . spending time together for the last time in our home.

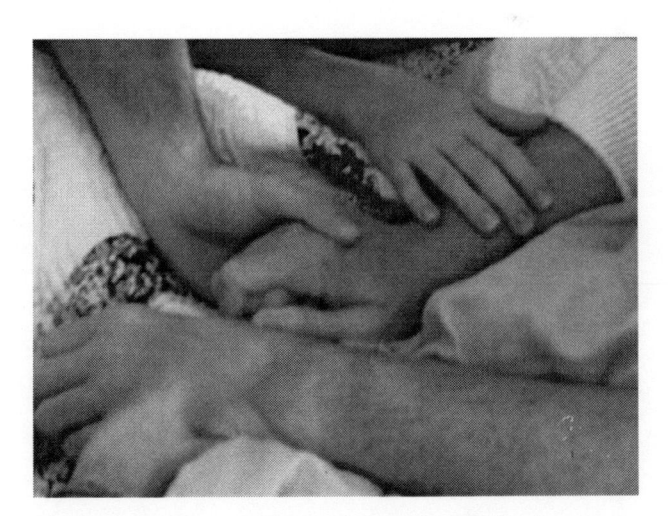

Bryan and Brittney holding Keith's hand, while I rub the other hand. This is the last day at home together before Keith was transported to Sterling House Assisted Living facility.

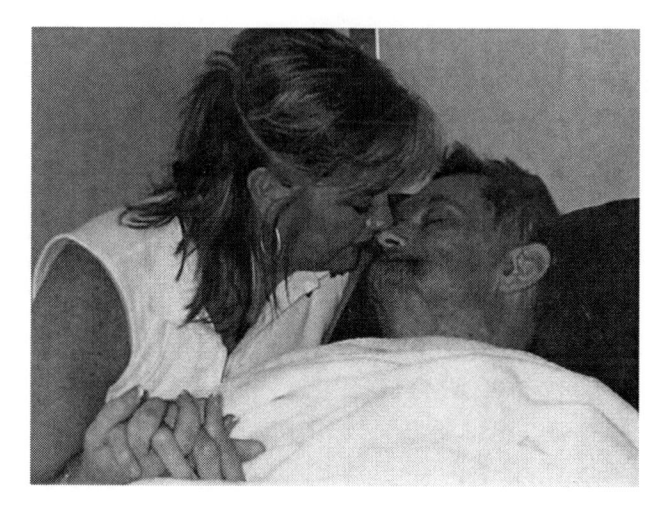

Me and Keith holding hands and sharing a tender moment the week before his death.

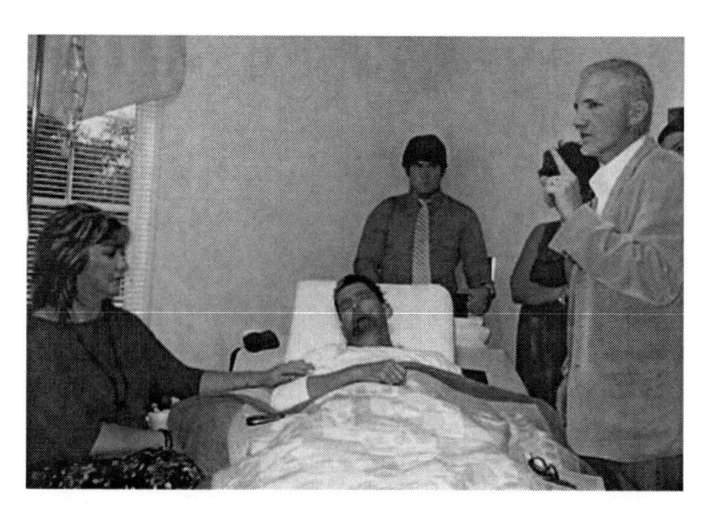

Easter Sunday morning service in Keith's room at Sterling House Assisted Living facility, led by John Thomas.

Payton and Mitchell Williams hugs Bryan after Easter Sunday morning service in Keith's room at Sterling House Assisted Living facility.

Chapter Five
Glimpses of Heaven

In the last days of Keith's life, after we moved him into Sterling House Assisted Living Facility, Keith began to "communicate" things he was beginning to see from heaven. I have come to understand and believe that as we slip from this world into heaven, the veil becomes transparent between both worlds. I fully believe that the Lord allows this so that He can show us that heaven is a beautiful, loving, and rewarding place. This communication brought comfort and peace and reassurance to all of the family and friends gathered around each day.

Colors

This was the first information about the hereafter that Keith shared with us. We were talking to him and engaging him in the conversation in the room when he suddenly pointed his hand out in front of him. Oddly enough, the only thing in that direction was a set of closet doors. We were puzzled, and we asked him if he needed something from the closet. He shook his head no and continued to point. I said, "What is it, Keith?"

He whispered to me, "Colors! Colors!"

At the time, we didn't understand. Later, we learned that in many people's account of the transition from this life into heaven as that veil is being lifted between the two worlds, they are embraced by many beautiful, vibrant, and comforting colors! I can only imagine! Beautiful!

It was an exciting yet surreal experience, knowing that Keith was beginning to share his glimpse into heaven. What anticipation and intrigue came over us, waiting expectantly on the next moment of communication from him. And it came several times after that. With each moment of communication, he sent much deeper messages to us.

People

During a quiet moment in that last week, I noticed Keith suddenly woke and stretched out his arm, pointing out in front of him. With my human eyes, all I could see was that he was pointing toward the closet in the room. I asked him if he needed something in the closet. He just continued pointing, as if to say, "Look! Look!" I suddenly realized he was seeing something with his eyes that was actually in heaven. I asked him, "Keith, what do you see?"

With as much strength as he could muster, he said, "People. People."

I said, "People? You see people?"

He nodded his head yes. I was starting to understand that his time was getting close. The Lord was sending loved ones to greet him for his time to cross over. At that moment, I said to him, "Keith, are those people there waiting for you?"

Once again, he nodded his head yes. Wow! At this moment, I received a peace or a release, and I rejoiced, knowing that the Lord had prepared the way for him and sent people to escort him to the gates of heaven!

Grandmamma

The day after he shared the fact that he was seeing people, he also kept pointing and saying "Grandmamma, grandmamma." I knew then that one of those people he saw was his grandmamma, who had passed away over ten years prior. That, too, was comforting to know she was among his loved ones waiting there to greet him.

Payoff

Of all the communication that Keith shared, this is the one that I am not 100 percent sure about what he was trying to tell me. One of those last days, he awoke and started gesturing with his hand (the same way you would gesture to say, "Go on!") But instead, he uttered under his breath, "Payoff," and he waited a few seconds and said again, "Payoff."

I was totally confused, and I asked my friend waiting at his bedside with him, "What does that mean?" The only thing I could rationalize was that he was telling me to "pay off everything," which I did later. We had always struggled financially, especially during the last seven years of his illness. I felt like the Lord was sending a message through him for us to pay off everything so that I could live life without all the financial struggles.

Live Life

Of all the messages that Keith communicated to us, this one left the most profound and lasting impact on our lives. He shared it with me on one of the quiet, rare afternoons when we didn't have a steady stream of friends and family hanging on to those last precious moments with Keith. It was just me and our friend Paula there, and we could have heard a pin drop it was so quiet. As Keith lay there asleep, I felt like joining him, because I was so exhausted at this point. All I wanted to do was curl up and sleep for days, but I couldn't do that because I didn't want to miss one second of Keith's last moments. Just as I was about to give in to the fatigue and fall asleep, Keith halfway opened his eyes and reached out to "brush his hand in a backward motion." He did that several times as he mumbled under his breath. I got up and went to his bedside, asking him to repeat what he had just mumbled. He did once again, but I could only understand an L sound. I then said, "Keith, honey, you are gonna have to speak louder. I can't understand you."

With a very labored and deep breath, he forced out the simple words, "*Live life!*" Those words were more profound than any I had heard from anybody in a long time. With those two simple words, I felt like he was saying, "I'm leaving this place," and, "I want you to live your life to its fullest without feeling guilty about moving on without me." In one instance, it was like he was saying, "This is it. It's over for me. I will be gone soon." And then in another instance, I felt he was saying, "You have my approval to move on with life. It's okay." I immediately began to weep, and then I sobbed. After I pulled myself together, I knew I had to tell the kids, because I felt that he wanted them to get that message too, that he wanted all of us to understand him. When they each came into the room that afternoon, I shared his message with them, and they, too, reacted that same way. To this day, we still reference Keith's command for our lives as we try to move on, enjoy life, and cherish every moment we have. Both the kids also vowed to have that statement engraved or memorialized so that it would follow them for the rest of their lives!

Throwing the Ball

One of these instances of communications that Keith portrayed during the last week happened when he slung his arm out in front of him time after time. At first, we could not figure out what that meant. Then I looked closely and realized he was holding his hands exactly the way he did when he was throwing a baseball. I asked him, "Keith, are you throwing ball with someone?"

He nodded his head yes! Then I just had to know with *whom* he was throwing ball. One by one, we began listing off names we knew had already gone to be with the Lord. One by one, he nodded his head no. We were puzzled. Who could it be?

About two days later, he started that same motion again. We went through another list of names with him, and we got the same results. We were frustrated that we could not resolve this moment of "communication between this world and heaven." We had figured out the rest, so why not this one?

Then two weeks after Keith passed away, I finally understood. I got it! I was reading a book someone gave me to help me through the grief. It was a small book titled *Heaven Is for Real*. In the book, this young boy describes to his parents his glimpse of heaven when he clinically died on an operating table. He told his parents that in heaven, he met his older sister (one that his parents had not told him had died at childbirth). The book told me about how that comment had brought comfort to his mother, now knowing that one day she would see her child again. In that moment, as I read that, it was like the Lord had sent this revelation to me, and it hit me like a lightning bolt! It answered two questions for me at one time! In between the birth of Brittney and Bryan, we had had a miscarriage, and I often wondered if I would ever know what that child was—boy or girl?—and if I would know it and if it would know me when I got to heaven? The answer was yes! But what did this have to do with Keith throwing a ball with someone during his last days? In that moment, I had an instant peace! And I literally cried out, "That's it! That's it! Keith has met our child at the gates of heaven and was throwing a ball with him! I know it.

I have *no doubt*," and I began to cry with joy, peace, and comfort, knowing that Keith was playing ball with our unborn child (who was now complete in the Lord) and that they were together in the presence of the Lord!

Psalm 126:2

*Our mouths were filled with laughter, our tongues with songs of **joy**. Then it was said among the nations, "The LORD has done great things for them."*

Chapter Six
Blessings of Easter

This day brought such bittersweet feelings. We knew it would be our last Easter together, but it turned out to be a special one, as any Easter should be to Christians. I wanted our family to celebrate this day with the same traditions and dedication as years past. And with the help of friends and family and our Sunday school class, it was exactly that . . . and more.

Even though we had to celebrate in Keith's room at Sterling instead of in the our church and home like every Easter for the past thirty years, the day turned out to be more touching and memorable than any other Easter in our lives, not just because of what was happening with Keith but because the Lord was *very present* in everything and everyone!

As a family, we decided to dress up just as if we would be attending church, even though we were just going to sit in that room with Keith. That was the way every Easter Sunday had been, and this Easter would be no different! We had already planned for our Sunday school class to come to us, because we couldn't be there at church. They wanted to honor the man who had led some of them in Sunday school for over twenty years. We were not sure what the turnout would be, but we knew that God would provide. And boy, did He!

As that gloomy, overcast morning began and the family all arrived, we began to prepare the small room for the members of our Sunday school class. I was already "on the edge," knowing this would be our last Easter with Keith, but as I walked out into the hallway where all the Sunday school members were waiting, I was so totally overwhelmed! I began to weep because of support and love shown that morning by all those Keith had taught in class for so many years. As we began to pack them into the room, we soon realized there was over fifty friends and family, not another inch of floor space to spare. I have never felt such a sense of love and reverence in one room in all my life!

As we began our final class together that day, the overcast skies outside developed into rain and lightning storms. How fitting that was on this final Easter Sunday together as we started our service with Keith in that packed room that the thunder and lightning crashed all around us, just as it did on the day of redemption! We welcomed those storms as part of God's blessing during these special, last moments together.

As John Thomas spoke the word inside, the Lord was speaking to us outside! Once John brought the message to a close, we began to sing, "Because He lives—" As we lifted our voices up in praise, there was a huge clap of thunder outside, and Keith slowly gained the strength to open his eyes. He slowly looked around the room and took in the sight and sound of the moment and then closed his eyes once again. It was a gift to everyone in that room that Keith could acknowledge their presence and support one last time! It was a powerful moment!

As John closed that special service in prayer, each person in that room came up and prayed over Keith and signed a prayer blanket that had been laid over him that morning. Then they each hugged Keith and said their last good-byes to him. It was a very emotional morning—a time of closure and letting go. Just as each friend began to exit the room and the mornings events began to calm down, so did the storms outside. It was almost as if the Lord had been saying, "I am here with you. Don't you hear me?"

Our very special and giving friend Mark Weakley, who is a fabulous cook and caterer, offered to cook our family a complete Easter dinner and bring it to us. Again, God provided. It was around noon, just about an hour after everyone had left from our special Easter service, when Mark brought in a complete meal with our usual Easter ham and all the sides. He helped make this Easter as normal as possible. We all picked a place around the room to eat, me, Brittney, and Bryan all picking a spot on each side of Keith's bed. Even though Keith wasn't communicating much at all at this point, we all continued to engage him in our conversation as we ate. Although Keith had basically stopped eating and drinking a couple of days before, we felt like he was partaking in the meal with us.

Brittney, Bryan, and I all had our last communication from Keith on this day, too. It was something we all needed for closure. Again, God provided. As we were eating that day, Keith opened his eyes and slightly lifted his head to focus on Bryan, who was sitting at the foot of the bed. Without saying a word, Keith lifted his hand, and in his last attempt to make us laugh, he sent a message by flashing a "love sign" to Bryan. Men don't get too mushy, but they shared this sign with one another so that they could say, "I love you," without saying the words! We all giggled as Bryan sent the signal back and said to Keith, "I love you too, Dad!" *That was Bryan's last moment with Keith.*

An hour or so after lunch, Brittney made her way again to Keith's bedside. She crawled up beside him and laid her head on his shoulder and began to talk to him. She shared with him what a great dad and a great role model he had been and how she felt so loved by him. And with all his strength, he whispered one last time to Brittney, "I love you!" *That was Brittney's moment.*

Later that afternoon in a rare moment of quiet time, only the kids and I were in the room with Keith. I went over and sat on the edge of the Keith's bed. I picked up his left arm, which he had lost all use of the weekend before, and I laid it over my legs. I then lay down over on his chest, and I, too, talked to Keith. I let him know all the ways he was special to me, and I thanked him for giving me two beautiful children and being a wonderful father to them. I thanked him for making me laugh throughout my life, and I thanked him for loving the Lord. I also told him that I was jealous that he was going to get to meet Jesus before I was. With tears streaming down my face, I knew that he could hear every word I said, but I did not expect him to respond. All of sudden, he raised his right arm (the only limb he still had use of) and began to stroke my hair and face. That was a moment I will always treasure, because in the last seven years of his illness, those intimate moments were few and far between. Also, he knew that rubbing my hair and face was one of the things I loved. I can't tell you how long we lay there sharing that moment, but for me, it felt like a lifetime. *That was my last moment with Keith.*

Escorted into Heaven

There were many signs of impending death that we had been warned about, each appearing more pronounced every day. I wanted to believe he would last another week, but my heart was telling me otherwise. I sensed the time was near. I felt it. That morning after Easter Sunday, I began telling those who came into the room that I felt like he only had a few days left, if even that long. All the signs were there. I just knew.

Shortly after 5:30 p.m., Keith's hospice nurse informed us that "it would not be long." As I began to brace myself for uncertain moments ahead, I also began to get the word out to everyone. As those next precious hours ticked away and I dealt with Brittney and Bryan grasping the reality of the moment, the room and halls filled with family and friends. I was amazed by the number of people who surrounded us in those last moments. As the time grew closer and signs became clearer, many there came into the room for a brief moment to touch him, kiss him, hug him, and say good-bye one last time. That room and hallway was so filled by such an overwhelming amount of love that you could literally sense the energy present. I fully believe it was that energy of love that carried me and the family into those last moments.

We began slowly gathering immediate family around the bed. Brittney was on one side, Bryan on the other side, I was at his feet, and his father, brother, family, and close friends filled in the gaps. Our amazing hospice nurse, Tamara, notified us that it was time.

With our pastor's leadership, we all sang "Because He lives" and then "Beulah Land," and at the urging of Keith's nephew, Dustin, we sang "Amazing Grace." On the second verse of that song, we sang Keith into heaven. Not just the family that was gathered around the bed sang, but *everyone* who filled the room and spilled out into the hallway also sang along with us. Not only did Keith have a heavenly choir of angels rejoicing over his homecoming, but at 10:25 p.m., he also had an earthly choir escorting him into heaven. It was the most amazingly powerful and beautiful experience I had ever had!

And once again, God proved that He was an on-time God, because the scripture of John 14:27 was given to me the day after Keith's funeral to give me reassurance that He would be with me in the uncertain days ahead.

John 14:27

*Peace I leave with you, my peace I give you. I do not give to you as the world gives.
Do not let your hearts be troubled and do not be afraid.*

Chapter Seven
Divine Assignment

So came the ending of a large chapter in our lives. Closure is often times difficult and scary to accept. It means there is a new chapter and a new plan for our lives. Whether you have been catapulted into this new life because of a tragedy, death, divorce, financial loss, or other major change, know that the Lord does have a plan for you. Even though you may have suffered, the Lord promised He would carry you. But did you take a look around and recognize His hand in the midst of your pain? We recognize those around us through the relationships we have with them. We know our parents by their love and affection for us, and we have faith that they will take care of us each day. It's the same when it comes to the love of our heavenly Father. He is there taking care of us every step of the way, no matter what we go through. You first must have *faith* to believe that He exists, that He is there, that He is real. Then when you call upon His name and *seek* His help, He will be there, whether you see Him clearly in that moment or not. Then you must have *hope* to wait expectantly that He is there to take care of you and that He has a plan for your life despite your circumstances. When you possess these three basic foundations in your relationship with God, you will recognize Him just as you recognize your own earthly father and mother.

It took that relationship with the Lord for me to recognize the plan He had for my life after Keith's death. His plan called for me to write this book. And let me tell you, it is written strictly on *faith*.

About a year and a half before I put these words on paper, I kept hearing a voice saying, "Lynn, write a book. Lynn, write a book. Lynn, write a book." I immediately thought, *'Are you talking to me? No! That's crazy. I am* not *going to write a book. I don't how to write a book'*. The voice kept speaking to me . . . again and again: "Lynn, write a book." At first, I ignored the voice. Then I began questioning and arguing with the Lord. At this time, I suspected that He was "calling me" on a mission, even though I didn't want to believe it. Needless to say, in the midst of everything going on with Keith, I truly could not understand how I would have the time, energy, or *knowledge* to write a book. I became increasingly irritated when He would not leave me alone and let this idea of a book go. As I argued with Him over this assignment, I came up with *one valid reason* that I thought would surely convince the Lord why He had chosen the wrong person as a writer. I remembered screaming out, *"This is ridiculous!* I am not going to write a book! Why would you want *me* to write a book, Lord? *I don't even like to read!"*

I thought that I had won *that* argument. (Yeah, right!). For months after that, every time I heard that voice telling me to write a book, I would ignore it and push it away. I had become so good at ignoring the voice that I don't recall hearing it for months after that. However, at the end of Keith's life, after the Lord had shown Himself over and over again, *that* voice returned *louder* and *stronger!*

This time, I had no doubt *who* was speaking to me. In my heart, I now knew that the Lord was calling *me* to this divine assignment. I knew that after everything that I had gone through, after everything that He had brought me through, after He had taken care of me and my family, I had no choice but to step out in faith and "accept the assignment." I had one last argument with Him, and I said, "This is impossible, I know *nothing* about writing a book. *I am not equipped to do this!* But okay, Lord. You win! I will write this book . . . even though I still think it's crazy. I'll write the book. You know I don't know the first thing about writing a book, how to put together a manuscript, how to go about finding a publisher, the legal details. Again, I think it is crazy. But here, it's in your hands. I'll do it!"

There. Done. Whew. Now what?

Ephesians 3:20-1

Now to Him who is able to do immeasurably more than all we ask or imagine, according to His power that is at work within us. To Him be glory in the Christ Jesus throughout all generations, forever and ever. Amen!

Within the coming days and weeks following Keith's death, the Lord began to work through me. Information and guidance began pouring out of me—the title of the book, the names of the chapters, the content of the preface, what the cover of the book would look like. Just with some guidance from the Lord, before I realized it, I had a publisher. I prayed over this assignment, and I knew that I needed a person to help guide me through that process, not just an online contact. I knew I wanted a publisher that would read the book and make sure it was theologically sound. Out of nowhere (or so I thought), I had been assigned a publishing consultant. He contacted me and said he wanted to talk to me personally and interview me (one answer to my prayer). And he even said that the interview was designed to make sure my book was . . . theologically sound! Just what I had prayed for! This was yet another confirmation that the Lord had complete control of this assignment. God is good!

Joy Comes in the Mourning

I was soon reminded of Luke 1:37, which says, "Nothing is impossible with God." That alone reaffirmed that even though I could not write this book, the Lord could write it through me. After I shared all of this with one of my friends at church, I said, "I am not equipped to do this."

She said, "Lynn, do you know who you sound like? Moses!"

I was stunned! But it drove home the point that even though I could not see with my earthly eyes how something bigger than myself could possibly happen, the Lord could use me as His instrument to accomplish the task at hand.

For the first time in my life, I understood what stepping out in complete trust, guidance, and faith in the Lord meant. James 2:22 states "You see that His faith and His actions were working together, and His faith was made complete by what He did." And if you combine faith with works, then you will see with your heavenly as well as your earthly eyes that *faith works!*

Thus, in my case, this book has come to fruition so the Lord can show others that if you first believe, then seek, and finally wait expectantly, He will be there in your times of darkness, trials, pains, and tragedies to love you and let you know that *you* . . . can have *joy in the mourning!*

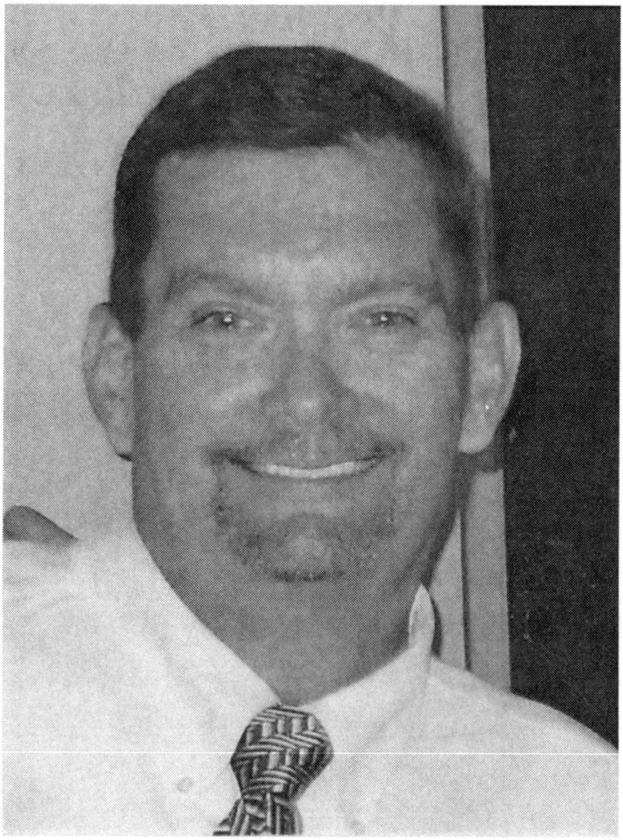

The Roman Road To Salvation

Do you have that special relationship with the Lord I have spoken of in the previous pages? If not, the Roman Road to salvation can guide you through the truths the Lord wants you to know.

Don't miss out on the miraculous plans the Lord has for you due to unbelief. Matthew 13:58 says "the Lord did not do miracles in their lives because of their lack of faith'. Place your trust in Him, and be prepared for God's grace upon your life and experience all the peace, and love, and hope, and joy the Lord intended for your life!

The first verse on the Romans Road to salvation is Romans 3:23:

"For all have sinned, and come short of the glory of God." We have all sinned. We have all done things that are displeasing to God. No one is innocent. Romans 3:10-18 gives a detailed picture of what sin looks like in our lives. "There is no one righteous, not even one; there is no one who understands; there is no one who seeks God. All have turned away, they have together become worthless; there is no one who does good, not even one."[b]

The second Scripture in the Romans Road is Romans 6:23:

This teaches us about the consequences of sin - "For the wages of sin is death; but the gift of God is eternal life through Jesus Christ our Lord." The punishment that we have earned for our sins is death. Not just physical death, but eternal death!

The third verse on the Romans Road to salvation continues with Romans 5:8:

"But God demonstrates His own love toward us, in that while we were still sinners, Christ died for us." Jesus Christ died for you, and for me! Jesus' death paid the price for our sins. Jesus' resurrection proves that God accepted Jesus' death as the payment for our sins.

The fourth step in the Romans Road is Romans 10:9:

"If you confess with your mouth Jesus as Lord, and believe in your heart that God raised Him from the dead, you will be saved." All we have to do is believe in Him, trusting His death as the payment for our sins - and we will be saved! Romans 10:13 says it again, "for everyone who calls on the name of the Lord will be saved." Jesus died to pay the penalty for our sins and rescue us from eternal death. Salvation, the forgiveness of sins, is available to anyone who will trust in Jesus Christ as their Lord and Savior.

The final aspect of the Romans Road is the results of salvation. Romans 5:1.

"Therefore, since we have been justified through faith we have peace with God through our Lord Jesus Christ." Romans 8:1

teaches us, "Therefore, there is now no condemnation for those who are in Christ Jesus." Because of Jesus' death on our behalf, we will never be condemned for our sins. Finally, we have a precious promise from God in Romans 8:38-39. "For I am convinced that neither death nor life, neither angels nor demons, neither the present nor the future, nor any powers, neither height nor depth, nor anything else in all creation, will be able to separate us from the love of God that is in Christ Jesus our Lord."

Are you ready to find salvation in the Lord and have that peace, and hope, and joy described throughout *Joy Comes In The Mourning*? If so, pray this simple prayer to declare to God that you are relying on Jesus Christ for your salvation. The words themselves will not save you. Only faith in Jesus Christ can provide salvation!

"God, I know that I have sinned against you and am deserving of punishment. But I believe Jesus Christ took the punishment on the cross that I deserve, so that through faith in Him I could be forgiven. I place my trust in You for salvation. I ask You right now to forgive me, and come into my heart. I want to receive you as my own personal Lord and Savior. Thank You for Your wonderful grace and forgiveness - the gift of eternal life! Amen!"

Halleluiah!!!

Did you know the angels in heaven are rejoicing right now over your decision? God's word says in Luke 15:10 "In the same way, I tell you, there is rejoicing in the presence of the angels of God over one sinner who repents."

Congratulations!!!

The Promises Of Joy

Deuteronomy 16:15

For the LORD your God will bless you in all your harvest and in all the work of your hands, and your joy will be complete.

Nehemiah 8:10

Nehemiah said, "Go and enjoy choice food and sweet drinks, and send some to those who have nothing prepared. This day is holy to our Lord.

Do not grieve, for the joy of the LORD is your strength."

Esther 9:22

...as the time when the Jews got relief from their enemies, and as the month when their sorrow was turned into joy and their mourning into a day of celebration.

Job 8:21

He will yet fill your mouth with laughter and your lips with shouts of joy.

Job 33:26

Then that person can pray to God and find favor with him, they will see God's face and shout for joy; he will restore them to full well-being.

Psalm 28:7
The LORD is my strength and my shield; my heart trusts in him, and he helps me.
My heart leaps for joy, and with my song I praise him.

Psalm 30:11
You turned my wailing into dancing; you removed my sackcloth and clothed me with joy.

Psalm 51:12
Restore to me the joy of your salvation and grant me a willing spirit, to sustain me.

Psalm 65:8
The whole earth is filled with awe at your wonders; where morning dawns, where evening fades, you call forth songs of joy.

Psalm 71:23
My lips will shout for joy when I sing praise to you— I whom you have delivered.

Psalm 126:5
Those who sow with tears will reap with songs of joy.

Isaiah 49:13

Shout for joy, you heavens; rejoice, you earth; burst into song, you mountains! For the LORD comforts his people and will have compassion on his afflicted ones.

Isaiah 51:11

Those the LORD has rescued will return. They will enter Zion with singing; everlasting joy will crown their heads. Gladness and joy will overtake them, and sorrow and sighing will flee away.

Isaiah 61:3
And provide for those who grieve in Zion—to bestow on them a crown of beauty instead of ashes, the oil of joy instead of mourning, and a garment of praise instead of a spirit of despair. They will be called oaks of righteousness, a planting of the LORD for the display of his splendor.

John 16:20
Very truly I tell you, you will weep and mourn while the world rejoices.
You will grieve, but your grief will turn to joy!

John 16:22
Now is your time of grief, but I will see you again and you will rejoice, and no one will take away your joy.

John 16:24
Until now you have not asked for anything in my name. Ask and you will receive, and your joy will be complete.

2 Corinthians 7:4
I have spoken to you with great frankness; I take great pride in you. I am greatly encouraged; in all our troubles my joy knows no bounds.

James 1:2
Consider it pure joy, my brothers and sisters, whenever you face trials of many kinds because you know that the testing of your faith produces perseverance . . . Blessed is the one who perseveres under trial because, having stood the test, that person will receive the crown of life that the Lord has promised to those who love him.

Joy

CPSIA information can be obtained at www.ICGtesting.com
Printed in the USA
LVOW122011270812

296218LV00002B/2/P